Kiss, Kiss

♥ by Jennifer Couëlle ♥ Illlustrated by Jacques Laplante
♥ Translated by Karen Simon

pajamapress

A

Kiss

is sweet

when 4 lips meet.

You can do it once,

or twice.

100 times is very nice.

If you have lots of love to send,

add  at the end.

Then you'll have... Kisses!

Most kisses are planted right on the cheek,

but blowing them is just fine, too.

They fly through the air and land on you.

They dry up your tears
              as quick as can be.

A kiss on the ear, a kiss on the nose
tickles you down to the tips of your toes.

When grownups kiss it may look sappy.

Well, they're in love—and very happy.

Kisses that say "Hi"

look just like those that say

"Goodbye"

In the morning,
and at noon.

Even underneath
the moon.

Good-night kisses on the head.
Hugs before we go to bed.

A morning kiss can feel so right—
like sunshine after
a rainy night.

Some kisses make noises:

big ones like...

Smooch!

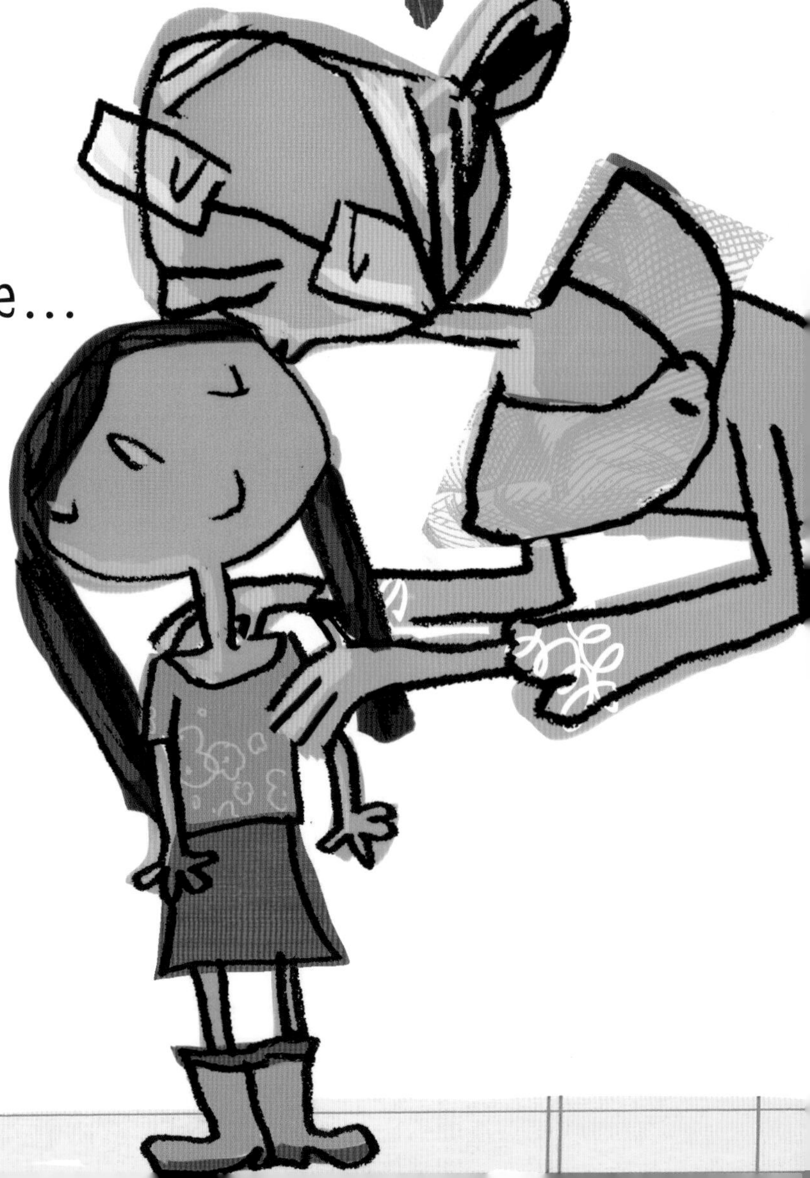

And little ones like...

peck!

Even kisses that are quick sometimes leave red marks that stick.

And kisses that are slurpy

are always kind of messy. They go

sshmuah!

Now a baby's kiss is wetter,

but it's still much better

than no kiss at all.

Because a day without kissing
has something missing.

But a shower of kisses

never misses.

I love

First published in the United States and Canada in 2015
Text copyright © 2015 Jennifer Couëlle
Illustrations copyright © 2015 Jacques Laplante
This edition copyright © 2015 Pajama Press Inc.
Translated from French by Karen Simon
First published in French by Dominique et compagnie.

10 9 8 7 6 5 4 3 2 1

www.pajamapress.ca   info@pajamapress.ca

Canada Council   Conseil des arts
for the Arts   du Canada

ONTARIO ARTS COUNCIL
CONSEIL DES ARTS DE L'ONTARIO
an Ontario government agency
un organisme du gouvernement de l'Ontario

Canadä

The publisher gratefully acknowledges the support of the Canada Council for the Arts and the Ontario Arts Council for its publishing program. We acknowledge the financial support of the Government of Canada through the Canada Book Fund (CBF) for our publishing activities.

Library and Archives Canada Cataloguing in Publication

Couëlle, Jennifer
[Bisou. English]
Kiss, kiss / words by Jennifer Couëlle ; pictures by Jacques Laplante
; translated by Karen Simon.
Translation of: Le bisou.
ISBN 978-1-927485-86-6 (bound)
I. Laplante, Jacques, 1965-, illustrator II. Simon, Karen, translator
III. Title. IV. Title: Bisou. English.
PS8605.O887B5713 2015   jC843'.6   C2015-902556-7

Publisher Cataloging-in-Publication Data (U.S.)

Couëlle, Jennifer, 1965 -
Kiss, kiss / words by Jennifer Couëlle ; pictures by Jacques Laplante ; translated by Karen Simon.
Originally published in French as: Le bisou.
[24] pages : color illustrations ; cm.
Summary: "In poetic language suitable for very young children, a joyful exploration of the different meanings of and ways of experiencing a kiss" - Provided by publisher.
ISBN-13: 978-1-927485-86-6
1. Kissing - Juvenile fiction. I. Jacques Laplante, 1965 - . II. Karen Simon, 1947 - . III. Title.
[E] dc23   PZ7.1.C684Ki 2015

Manufactured by Qualibre Inc./Print Plus
Printed in China

Pajama Press Inc.
181 Carlaw Ave. Suite 207 Toronto, Ontario Canada, M4M 2S1

Distributed in Canada by UTP Distribution
5201 Dufferin Street Toronto, Ontario Canada, M3H 5T8

Distributed in the U.S. by Ingram Publisher Services
1 Ingram Blvd. La Vergne, TN 37086, USA

For Katia Belsito
–J. C.

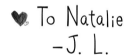 To Natalie
–J. L.

Angkor Wat

UNEARTHING ANCIENT WORLDS

Alison Behnke

Twenty-First Century Books • Minneapolis

Twenty-First Century Books
A division of Lerner Publishing Group, Inc.
241 First Avenue North
Minneapolis, MN 55401 U.S.A.

Website address: www.lernerbooks.com

Library of Congress Cataloging-in-Publication Data

Behnke, Alison.
   Angkor Wat / by Alison M. Behnke.
     p.   cm. — (Unearthing ancient worlds)
   Includes bibliographical references and index.
   ISBN 978-0-8225-7585-6 (lib. bdg. : alk. paper)
   1. Angkor Wat (Angkor)—Juvenile literature. 2. Cambodia—Antiquities—Juvenile literature.
I. Title.
   DS554.98.A5B4 2009
   959.6'02—dc22   2007050269

Manufactured in the United States of America
1 2 3 4 5 6 – PA – 14 13 12 11 10 09

TABLE OF CONTENTS

This aerial view of Angkor Wat shows the main temple complex, as well as its moat and front gate. Angkor Wat is located in Siem Reap Province in Cambodia. Siem Reap City provides hotels, restaurants, and transportation for tourists.

INTRODUCTION

In 1860 a French explorer and scientist named Henri Mouhot made his way through the dense Cambodian jungle. In addition to being a traveler, Mouhot was a natural history scholar. He worked for Britain's Royal Geographical Society and for the Zoological Society of London. These groups had sent him to Southeast Asia to explore and to collect samples of local plant life.

This region is covered with thick jungles, rich in plants and animals. The area also includes modern-day Thailand (then known as Siam), Laos, and Vietnam. By 1860 he had arrived in the small nation of Cambodia.

As Mouhot trekked through Cambodia, he heard rumors of huge stone ruins hidden deep in the jungle. Deciding to see these sights for himself, he had a local guide take him there. This guide showed him the remains of a great city. Many of its buildings lay in ruins. But one giant temple still stood tall and impressive: Angkor Wat. Its five massive stone towers rose out of the jungle toward the sky. Mouhot was amazed at its size and its beauty.

Henri Mouhot around 1850

The ruins and temple Mouhot saw are in a region called Angkor. Angkor lies on a flat plain in northern Cambodia. To its south is a large lake called Tonle Sap. The Kulen Hills rise out of the jungle north of Angkor.

This area was the center of a civilization that thrived between A.D. 800 and the late 1300s. It was called the Khmer Empire. For hundreds of years, Angkor was home to the empire's rulers and other high-ranking people. It served as the empire's capital area and was a busy hub of Khmer culture. It was also the empire's religious center. At first, Khmer kings and their subjects followed Hinduism. Later, many practiced Buddhism. Both of these faiths came to the region from India. The city's largest temple, Angkor Wat, served both religions at different times.

Then, around the late 1300s, the Khmer Empire collapsed. Angkor was nearly abandoned. The thick, fast-growing Cambodian jungle began

FAST FACTS ABOUT ANGKOR AND ANGKOR WAT

- Angkor was the capital of the ancient Khmer Empire. It was the home of the Khmer rulers. It was also a center of culture, business, and religion. The Angkor area includes many temples and royal buildings.

- The most famous building in Angkor is Angkor Wat. This great temple is one of the largest ancient structures in the world. It began as a Hindu temple when it was built in the first half of the 1100s. Later, it was also used for Buddhist worship.

- Angkor first arose in the early A.D. 800s. The Khmer Empire and Angkor reached their peak in the 1100s and 1200s.

- Experts think that during the Khmer Empire's strongest period, Angkor held a population of up to one million people.

- Angkor mysteriously collapsed sometime between the 1300s and 1400s. Historians are not sure why Angkor fell. But they do have some ideas. Some believe that Cambodia's climate changed dramatically. This change then led to farming and food supply problems. Other historians think that the area's population simply grew too large. The land and its farms could no longer support so many people. Finally, in 1431, Thai armies attacked and conquered the weakened Angkor.

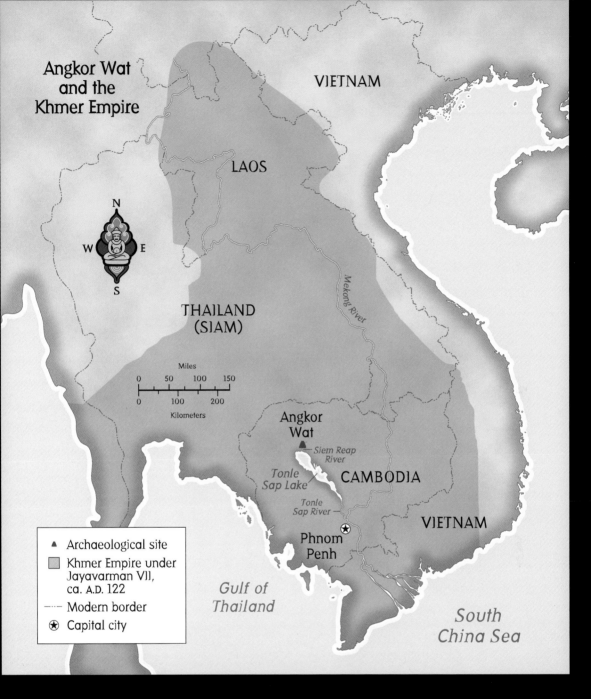

Angkor Wat and the Khmer Empire

VIETNAM

LAOS

N
W   E
S

THAILAND
(SIAM)

Mekong River

Miles
0   50   100   150
0   100   200
Kilometers

Angkor
Wat
▲
— Siem Reap
River

Tonle
Sap Lake

CAMBODIA

Tonle
Sap River —

Phnom ✪
Penh

VIETNAM

Gulf of
Thailand

South
China Sea

▲ Archaeological site
▨ Khmer Empire under
   Jayavarman VII,
   ca. A.D. 122
---- Modern border
✪ Capital city

to swallow up the area's buildings and temples. Even the great temple,
Angkor Wat, showed signs of age and decline.

When Mouhot arrived, most of the buildings at Angkor had fallen into
the jungle's grip. But even the thick vines and grasping tree roots could not
hide how amazing the place was. Mouhot and hundreds of later visitors,
students, and archaeologists spent many years researching and restoring
Angkor Wat and other buildings at this great site.

This illustration shows the main entrance to Angkor Wat shortly after its rediscovery. Jungle plants crowd the main road and cover many statues and small structures. The image appeared in an 1873 book about French explorations in Southeast Asia.

CHAPTER one

"THE WORK OF GIANTS"

In January 1860, Henri Mouhot is deep in Cambodia's northern jungle. On his mission to explore regions in Southeast Asia, he has come across a huge ancient city. At its heart is the great temple Angkor Wat.

Mouhot spends three weeks at Angkor. He speaks to the local people. He asks what they know about this amazing place. Who built it? How old is it?

Mouhot doesn't get answers to all of his questions. Some people tell him myths and wild stories about the area and its past. Some say that Angkor Wat is the "work of giants."

"The work of giants! The expression would be very just, if used figuratively, in speaking of these [remarkable] works, of which no one who has not seen them can form any adequate idea."

—Henri Mouhot, 1860s

But Mouhot does learn that the temple and other buildings have been here for as long as anyone can remember. And he writes careful notes about what he sees and hears. He draws sketches of the buildings.

PAST TRAVELERS

Mouhot does not realize that he is not the first European person to view these awesome sights. Traders and missionaries (religious workers) from Europe had begun arriving in the area in the 1500s. Antonio da Magdalena was a Portuguese friar (a member of a Catholic religious group) who came to the area in 1586. He saw the temple and some of the other buildings at Angkor.

After his visit, Magdalena told a Portuguese historian named Diogo do Couto about what he had seen. Couto then wrote down these stories. He wrote that the place is "so strange that one can hardly describe it with a pen, nor can one compare it to any other monument in the world." But these records were not published outside of Asia until many decades later.

"[Angkor] has towers and decoration and all the refinements which the human genius can conceive of. . . . The temple is surrounded by a moat, and access is by a single bridge, protected by two stone tigers so grand and fearsome as to strike terror into the visitor."

—Diogo do Couto, writing about Antonio da Magdalena's 1586 visit to Angkor

During the next few hundred years, others visit Cambodia and Angkor. Quite a few missionaries arrive during the 1600s. Most of them are from Spain and Portugal. In 1850 a French missionary named Charles-Émile Bouillevaux comes to the region. He spends two days at Angkor. Bouillevaux then publishes writings about his visit.

For many years, no one outside Cambodia has paid much attention to any of these reports. Most people have never even heard of Angkor. A few rumors about the place do spread to Europe. People in Europe tell tales of mysterious lost cities and monuments in the jungle. These stories usually assume that ancient Romans or Greeks must have built these sites.

Henri Mouhot changes all that forever. His visit turns out to be the beginning of many years of study and work at Angkor. During his trip, Mouhot writes a diary about what he sees. He describes the region and

The Family Business

Exploring ran in Mouhot's family—or, at least, his wife's family. Mouhot was married to a niece of Mungo Park. Park was a Scottish adventurer who explored Africa's Niger River in the early 1800s.

its temple. Even just a glimpse of the buildings at Angkor is stunning, he says. They are "ruins of such grandeur . . . that, at the first view, one is filled with profound admiration, and cannot but ask what has become of this powerful [people], so civilized, so enlightened, the authors of these gigantic works."

In 1861 Mouhot catches a fever. He dies in Laos. But fortunately, he leaves behind his work for others to learn from. A servant of Mouhot takes the explorer's diary to Bangkok, a city in Siam (Thailand). Eventually someone sends these writings back to France. And within a few years, Mouhot's writings on Angkor appear as a book in France.

Mouhot's book is called *Travels in Siam, Cambodia and Laos*. It includes many drawings of Angkor and its buildings. These detailed sketches catch people's imagination in France and other parts of Europe. So do his vivid descriptions of the site. For example, Mouhot writes about the eerie mood at Angkor when he first sees it. He says, "Hardly a sound echoes but the roar of tigers, the harsh cry of elephants and . . . wild stags." He goes on, "One of these temples . . . [could] take an honorable place beside our most beautiful buildings. It is grander than anything left to us by Greece or Rome."

COLONIAL DAYS

Soon after Mouhot's death, France begins to have a new and stronger influence in Cambodia. France had been founding many colonies and protectorates during this time. Colonies and protectorates are countries or regions that outside powers or nations control. France has already claimed territory in Vietnam and Laos. And in 1863, France makes Cambodia into another French protectorate.

In 1866 French officials become worried about their control in Southeast Asia. Great Britain is also founding colonies in the region. The

French government puts together a group called the Mekong Exploration Commission. It is formed to help protect France's territory and perhaps lead to France taking over greater areas. Ernest Doudart de Lagrée leads the commission. He and his team of five men are supposed to explore the Mekong River. Through this exploration, they hope to find a way to claim more territory. They are also on the lookout for valuable resources and for an easy route to China.

As the men travel along the river, they record what they see and find. A young man in the group named Francis Garnier makes careful maps of the area. Another group member, Louis Delaporte, is the commission's official artist. He sketches the people and places that the group sees along the journey.

The View from China

About one hundred years before the Khmer civilization fell, a Chinese visitor arrived at Angkor. Zhou Daguan traveled to the area in 1296. He spent about one year there. Fortunately for historians, Zhou wrote a lot about what he saw at Angkor. He described Khmer culture and life. Zhou wrote, "When the king goes out, troops are at the head of [his] escort; then come flags, banners, and music. Palace women . . . with flowers in their hair, hold candles in their hands, and form a troupe. Even in broad daylight, the candles are lighted."

Zhou also said that "ministers and princes are mounted on elephants, and in front of them one can see . . . their innumerable red umbrellas."

Zhou went on to describe the ruler himself and his grand entrance. "Behind them comes the [king], standing on an elephant, holding his sacred sword in his hand. The elephant's tusks are encased in gold."

In addition to Zhou, other Asian visitors also saw and described Angkor before Mouhot's arrival. In the 1630s, a Japanese visitor named Kenryo Shimano made a detailed drawing of Angkor Wat's layout. Other Chinese travelers followed in Zhou's footsteps and visited Angkor.

Ernest Doudart de Lagrée was born in France in 1823. He was a commander in the French navy and fought in the Crimean War (1853–1856) before leading the Mekong Exploration Commission.

During their travels, Lagrée and his team reach Angkor. They arrive in June of 1866 and spend one week in the ancient city. Like Mouhot, they view the site's great buildings with wonder. Delaporte makes careful drawings of these buildings and their architecture.

WORTH A THOUSAND WORDS

While the Mekong Exploration Commission does its work, another artistic traveler makes a trip to Cambodia. Mouhot's book has inspired many people. One of them is a Scottish man named John Thomson. Like Mouhot, Thomson works for the Royal Geographical Society. But his specialty is photography. He has already traveled in Asia taking pictures. After he reads Mouhot's descriptions of Angkor, Thomson decides to go to Cambodia to view the site for himself.

Thomson reaches Cambodia in 1866. He spends two weeks in Angkor. He takes more than fifty pictures of the region and especially of Angkor Wat. Thomson publishes these photos in 1867 in a book called *Antiquities of Cambodia*. His pictures spark even more outside interest in Angkor. More travelers and explorers come to Cambodia. They want to see these amazing ruins for themselves.

Photographer Emile Gsell took this picture in 1866. He accompanied the Mekong Exploration Commission on two different trips. He also opened the first photography studio in the city of Saigon, in modern-day Vietnam.

CHAPTER two

EXPLORING THE PAST

By 1868 people in France, Great Britain, and beyond have read Mouhot's writings on Angkor and seen Thomson's pictures of it. Interest in this ancient city and its treasures keeps growing.

Meanwhile, the Mekong Exploration Commission's work continues. The group's leader, Lagrée, dies in 1868. But the rest of the team keeps researching and recording details about the site. In 1873 they publish a report about what they have found. The report includes maps by Francis Garnier and many drawings by Louis Delaporte.

In addition to creating these valuable drawings, Delaporte ships some Khmer artwork back to France. He takes statues and other pieces of sculpture home with him. People in Europe, who have never seen Angkor, marvel at these works.

A DEAD LANGUAGE COMES TO LIFE

Many of the visitors to Angkor Wat see fascinating and detailed carvings in the temple's walls and pillars. Some of these carvings are writings called inscriptions. Most of these inscriptions are in the ancient language of Sanskrit. For many years, no one has been able to translate them. More

Sanskrit inscriptions decorate many of the walls in Angkor. Many record the history of the kings who built the temples.

than two thousand years ago, Sanskrit was the language used by people in India and other parts of Southeast Asia. But over time, most people stopped speaking the language. Eventually they used it only in writing. Finally, the language died out almost completely. By the 1800s, very few people in the world still understand Sanskrit. But scholars in Europe have been studying the language and working to crack its code. Researchers at Angkor Wat and other parts of Angkor hope that one day soon they will know what the many inscriptions say.

In 1879 a Dutch man named Hendrik Kern comes to Angkor. Kern has studied Sanskrit. He is the first visitor to Angkor who can read most of the carved writings that cover Angkor's walls, pillars, and doors.

A few years later, two Frenchmen, Auguste Barth and Abel Bergaigne, visit Angkor. Like Kern, they are Sanskrit scholars. They work to translate more than one thousand carved inscriptions. This work helps researchers learn much more about Khmer history and Angkor's rulers.

French Indochina

In 1887 France combined its territory in Vietnam, Laos, and Cambodia to form a bigger protectorate called Indochina.

Lucien Fournereau visits Angkor in 1887. Fournereau is a French architect. His knowledge of building styles and methods gives him a different understanding of Angkor. He carefully draws the layouts and floor plans of some of the buildings. He also makes drawings of what some buildings might have looked like when they were first built. These drawings add even more to people's knowledge about Angkor.

"Angkor the Great"

Word about Angkor kept spreading. Frank Vincent Jr., an American, visited Angkor in 1872. He went on to write a book called *The Land of the White Elephant: Sights and Scenes in South-Eastern Asia*. This work was one of the first books to introduce most Americans to Angkor. Vincent wrote about reaching the site for the first time. "We passed quickly and silently along a narrow but good road cut through the dense . . . forest." He goes on, "Suddenly emerging from the woods, we saw a little way off . . . across a pond filled with lotus plants, a long row of columned galleries, and beyond . . . three or four immense pagodas, built of a dark-grey stone. And my heart almost bounded into my mouth . . . for we were then at the very portals of the famous old 'City of Monasteries', and not far distant was Angkorthom—Angkor the Great."

In 1874 the *New York Times* published an article about Angkor Wat. It printed a description of the site by Vincent. He wrote, "The outer wall . . . is built of sandstone, with gateways upon each side, which are handsomely carved with figures of gods and dragons." Vincent went on to say that a person could spend weeks looking at these wonderful and varied pictures. He wrote, "You see warriors riding upon elephants and in chariots, foot soldiers with shield and spear, boats [and] trees."

Vincent said that seeing Angkor Wat was an amazing experience. He summed it up by saying, "The wonder of the temple is beautiful and romantic as well as impressive and grand . . . it must be seen to be understood and appreciated."

As time goes on, Angkor's visitors begin to realize that Angkor Wat and the nearby buildings are just a few of those that exist in the area. Many more ruins lie throughout the region. Some are actually beyond Cambodia's borders, in parts of Laos and Siam.

Around this time, a French explorer and archaeologist named Étienne Aymonier begins work in Angkor. He has been employed by France's government in Cambodia for a number of years. But his true specialty is the area's ancient languages. Like Kern, Aymonier can read Sanskrit. He keeps working on translating Angkor's inscriptions. Aymonier also starts to make a list of the temples and other structures in the Angkor region.

A NEW FRENCH CONNECTION

Soon a new organization gets involved in Angkor. It is a French group called L'École Française d'Extrême-Orient (EFEO). In English its name means "the French School of the Far East." The EFEO begins in 1898. Its headquarters are in the neighboring country of Vietnam. The EFEO's workers focus on studying Asian archaeology, history, and society. The EFEO sends archaeologists, scholars, and other workers around Asia to study different sites.

Some of these people come to the city of Angkor. They begin researching the Khmer Empire's history. They study the area's archaeology. They make many careful drawings of Angkor's ruins. And EFEO archaeologists take notes that describe the site and its many buildings.

Around the beginning of the 1900s, an EFEO member, Étienne-Edmond Lunet de Lajonquière, comes to work at Angkor. He takes over Aymonier's project of recording the region's ancient structures. Lajonquière continues documenting Khmer sites around Cambodia and also in neighboring countries. He expands Aymonier's list. Lajonquière even takes this project a step further. He and a team of helpers begin writing careful descriptions of every building and monument at Angkor—no matter how small. They also include maps of many sites. This work goes slowly and steadily. It takes the group seven years to finish. But at the end of this time, they have a list

Naming Angkor
The name *Angkor* comes from the Sanskrit word *nagara*, meaning "capital city."

Étienne-Edmond Lunet de Lajonquière (right) pauses on a trek through the Cambodian jungle. Explorers had to wade across swamps and cut paths through the jungle to reach Angkor Wat.

of 910 individual monuments. This detailed list is published in a set of three books between 1902 and 1911. It becomes a very important reference work for future workers and scholars at Angkor.

Another EFEO worker, Victor Goloubew, is a Russian who has studied art and archaeology. He also has a special interest in Asian history. In the 1920s, Goloubew begins taking aerial photographs of Angkor from airplanes flying over Cambodia. These images from the air give people more information about Angkor's layout and size. They give them a new perspective on how the pieces of Angkor fit together. Goloubew and other archaeologists use these images to learn more about Angkor's history and architecture.

Other EFEO workers look at the carvings and the inscriptions. They continue to learn things from this art and these writings. As they gather more information, they also begin to piece together the story of Angkor.

A LONG-AGO KINGDOM

Many of Angkor's inscriptions describe Khmer rulers from hundreds of years ago. Even before these kings came to power, Khmer-speaking people had lived in the Angkor region and beyond for many centuries. As early as the A.D. 100s, they were beginning to form villages. They raised crops and animals. Over time, many small kingdoms arose. Each had its own ruler. These kingdoms sometimes struggled for power. Neighboring groups, from Java and the Malay Peninsula, often managed to seize control of Khmer areas.

The inscriptions on Angkor's ruins tell historians that many things changed when a ruler named Jayavarman II took power. In A.D. 802, this prince declared that he was the universal ruler over all the Khmer people. He unified the many small realms in the region to form a single Khmer Empire. At the same time, he claimed Khmer independence from Java and outside rule. Jayavarman II also declared that he was a god-king. Many earlier Cambodian rulers had taken on this title. They claimed that higher powers chose and guided them.

Jayavarman II centered his empire in the region that later became known as Angkor. Over the years, Khmer workers cleared the jungle from huge areas of land. They made the land usable for farming. And they began to build palaces and temples.

"King of the Kings of Cambodia, glorious like the sun, whose eyes were like lotus flowers. . . . With a blow of his left arm he once killed an elephant."

—an Angkor inscription describing the Khmer king Yasovarman 1, who ruled from about 890 to 910

Inscriptions at Angkor describe Jayavarman II's important declaration and his reign. Historians call this the beginning of the Classic Period, or the Angkor Period. The archaeologists working at Angkor also believe that about this same time, the Khmer people began using stone for their buildings. Before, they had used wood. But by the time the EFEO arrives in Angkor, the wood is long gone. It has rotted away over the years. Only great stone structures such as Angkor Wat remain.

Carved writings on the walls of Angkor's buildings also describe many leaders following Jayavarman II. In the early 900s, a king named Yasovarman I set up a capital city in Angkor called Yasodharapura. In Sanskrit the name *Yasodharapura* means "Holy City."

In the late 1100s, the powerful king Jayavarman VII built a new capital called Angkor Thom. Angkor Thom lies within the larger Angkor area, not far from Angkor Wat.

These rulers also expanded the empire. At its peak in the late 1100s and early 1200s, the Khmer Empire covered much more than modern Cambodia. It included parts of present-day Laos, Thailand, Myanmar (also known as Burma), and Vietnam. Over the years, Khmer workers cleared the jungle from huge areas of the central Angkor region. They made more land usable for farming. And they built many palaces and temples.

But even as Angkor and the Khmer Empire thrived in some ways, they also faced challenges. Power struggles erupted within the kingdom. Enemies on the outside also attacked. Champa, a kingdom located in modern Vietnam, was a major threat. The empire began to weaken seriously in 1218 when the ruler Jayavarman VII died. In 1431 armies from a Thai kingdom called Ayutthaya attacked and conquered Angkor. Soon afterward, the entire Angkor region and its kingdom seem to have crumbled quite quickly. Some historians believe that this collapse began even earlier. The fall of the Khmer Empire may have happened as long ago as the mid to late 1300s.

Even after this decline, Angkor did not empty out completely. Angkor Wat itself stayed especially lively. Buddhist monks (religious men) remained there and still bustled to and fro. Worshippers still visited to pray and pay their respects. But most of the area's other buildings fell into ruin and decay.

This sculpture of Jayavarman VII shows the king meditating. Archaeologists found the statue at Angkor Thom and later moved it to the national museum in Phnom Penh, the capital of Cambodia.

Flowers and scarves decorate a statue of the Hindu god Vishnu at Angkor Wat.
Worshippers bring sticks of incense and burn them in the pot of rice at the statue's feet.

CHAPTER three

ARTS AND ARCHAEOLOGY

Workers and archaeologists at Angkor continue to clean and restore the region's buildings. They also keep studying the art and engravings they find there. Piece by piece, these works add to experts' knowledge about the site, the region, its people, and how they lived.

BUILDING TO THE HEAVENS

One important part of this story is the religion of Angkor's people. Knowing more about Khmer faith helps historians explain why its people built some buildings the way they did.

Many Khmer people were Hindus, following the religion of Hinduism. Hinduism became a major religion in India in about the 100s B.C., but it has much older roots. Hindus believe in many gods and goddesses. These beings influence many parts of human life. Two of the most important Hindu gods are Shiva and Vishnu. They both appear in many images at Angkor.

As time passed, some rulers at Angkor began following Buddhism. This religion began in India. A monk named Siddhartha Gautama (Buddha) founded the religion in the 500s B.C. Buddhism had reached Angkor by the A.D. 900s. Leaders there liked the new religion, and it was firmly in place

Priests dressed this statue of Buddha in a saffron-colored monk's robe. The statue sits in the Bayon temple group.

when Zhou Daguan arrived in 1296. Zhou described Buddhist monks at Angkor, saying that they "shave their heads, wear yellow robes, and bare their right shoulder." These monks became a powerful group in Khmer society. And the religion's central figure of Buddha also began appearing in Angkor's art.

Each Khmer king built grand temples and palaces in Angkor. The kings created these buildings partly to show how powerful they were. They also wanted to honor and please the gods. For example, in 879 workers for the ruler Indravarman I built a Hindu temple called Preah Ko. This temple's name means "Sacred Bull." It honors a holy bull linked to the god Shiva. The later king, Jayavarman VII, oversaw the creation of a Buddhist temple group called the Bayon in the late 1100s and early 1200s.

But neither of these two rulers built Angkor's finest temple, Angkor Wat. The king Suryavarman II, who ruled from about 1113 until 1150, ordered workers to make a grand Hindu temple honoring the god Vishnu. Angkor Wat took more than thirty-five years to build.

As Khmer builders created these temples, the Hindu faith deeply influenced their work. They began designing religious complexes called Temple Mountains. This style of architecture symbolizes the mythical Mount Meru. According to Hindu beliefs, gods and goddesses live on this holy mountain. When Hindu architects built major temples at Angkor, they designed them to represent parts of Mount Meru and the surrounding area. Some Buddhist architects also used a version of the Temple Mountain idea.

ANGKOR WAT: JEWEL OF THE KHMER EMPIRE

Angkor Wat is a wonderful example of the Temple Mountain design. The temple has five huge towers. Each one represents one of Mount Meru's peaks. These towers rise out of a larger pyramid-shaped temple that stands for the whole mountain. Walls and a huge moat around the temple represent other mountain ranges and the ocean around Mount Meru.

"Angkor Wat staggers the imagination. One thinks of the vast hordes of laborers who [made] its great stone blocks and under the tropical sun [raised] them into position . . . the masons carving it from top to bottom like a tapestry, and the king watching this creation of his will slowly growing through long years."

—L. J. Robbins,
writing in the *New York Times,* 1930

Angkor Wat is an amazing work of Khmer architecture. It shows that symmetry and repetition were very important to Khmer design. The same shapes and patterns appear over and over. And Angkor Wat is much more than a temple. It is really a mini-city in itself. It is a whole complex of buildings on a large piece of land. It is also very well preserved compared to most of the other temples and buildings in Angkor.

Going from the outside in, archaeologists and workers at Angkor first reach Angkor Wat's huge moat. This waterway is more than 600 feet (183 meters) wide. A causeway (low bridge) stretches across the water. It reaches a small terrace and gateway through a large outer wall that stands almost 15 feet (4.6 m) high. In all, the area within this outer wall is about 200 acres (81 hectares).

The terrace and its gateway mark the entrance through the wall. This gateway is not just a simple door. It is a building in itself, decorated with carvings and statues. This type of fancy entryway is called a *gopura*. Three towers rise above this gopura, but the tops of the towers have begun to crumble and fall.

Inside the gate and the wall, the causeway becomes a raised walkway. A railing carved to look like a snake lines each side of the

walkway as it crosses the grounds. Trees and jungle plants cover much of this area. Not far beyond the gate, the walkway passes between two fairly small buildings called libraries. These buildings may or may not have once held books or papers. They were probably used mainly for worship. Beyond the libraries are two shallow pools.

As the walkway nears the main temple, it widens into a large, cross-shaped terrace. This area is called the Terrace of Honor. Carved lions and other statues decorate it. Just a few steps away stands another magnificent gopura. This gate passes through a covered hallway called a gallery. Four long galleries surround the central temple area. The inner

A brick causeway *(left)* crosses the moat at Angkor Wat. This picture shows the main temple in the distance beyond the elaborate gate. The moat draws water from the Siem Reap River.

A monk crosses the upper terrace at Angkor Wat. Carvings cover the walls and columns of the gallery surrounding the terrace.

wall of each gallery is solid. On the side facing the moat, the galleries are open. Columns and pillars lining this outer side hold up the gallery roof. Three other gopuras break through this set of galleries, one on each of the rectangle's sides.

These galleries are famous for their beautiful and detailed artwork. Khmer artists carved the stone walls to create three-dimensional pictures called reliefs. In the main Angkor galleries, these reliefs are about 6.5 feet (2 m) high. In all, these four large galleries hold about 12,900 square feet (1,198 sq. m) of carved artwork.

This set of galleries makes up the first and lowest level of the main temple. Beyond it are several open-air courtyards. Two more libraries also lie within this area. And at the western end of the temple is a cross-shaped set of galleries. Steps from these galleries connect this lowest level of the main temple with the second level above.

Upstairs, galleries line the edges of the second level and gopuras mark the entrances. Additional courtyards and two more libraries lie inside.

Finally, twelve separate stairways lead upward to the third and highest level of Angkor Wat. In the Khmer era, this level was only open to the king and the highest-ranking priest. Four of Angkor's main five towers mark the corners of the temple's third level. Like the lower tiers of the complex, this area contains courtyards and gopuras. And in the very center, Angkor Wat's tallest and largest tower rises above the temple's central shrine.

As the archaeologists study Angkor Wat and its layout, they gather many clues to the past. For example, the temple faces the west. But most other Khmer temples face the east. Some historians think that Angkor Wat's design—looking westward toward the setting sun—suggests a connection between this site and death. They think that Angkor Wat may have been a tomb for the king Suryavarman II, as well as a place of worship. But others believe that it faces west

Steep staircases lead to one of the five towers at Angkor Wat.

This relief sculpture from Angkor Wat shows Suryavarman II relaxing on his throne.

"He had hardly reached his adult years before he desired supreme power. He rose up against the king with an army and during a battle he leapt on to the royal elephant and there with his own hands struck down the king."

—an Angkor inscription describing Suryavarman II, who ruled from about 1113 to 1150

because it was dedicated to the god Vishnu. Vishnu is associated with the west.

Experts also learn more from faint outlines and indentations on the grounds of Angkor Wat. These clues show that roads once crisscrossed the land around the central temple. The historians think that older buildings once stood here. These buildings were probably made of wood. They must have rotted away after years in the heat and humidity. But historians think that one of these other buildings was a royal palace.

WHAT A RELIEF

Like the carved writings throughout the Angkor region, the area's many reliefs help teach the researchers about Angkor's past. And like the inscriptions, some show events from the lives of kings. But others show images of daily life during the Khmer Empire's peak. Reliefs at the Bayon temple complex are especially helpful. They give the archaeologists a lot of information. For example, the Bayon reliefs show how Angkor's ancient residents dressed. They also show specific scenes such as people shopping for food at a market, eating, and playing games. Still others show scenes of warfare.

The Cambodian jungle surrounding Angkor is rich with wildlife. This wildlife appears in much of the art at Angkor. This bas-relief carving from Angkor Wat shows villagers working while monkeys and peacocks climb in the branches overhead.

Some reliefs at Angkor teach the researchers more about Khmer religious beliefs. Many show popular stories from Hindu and Buddhist legends. One of the grandest and most impressive of these reliefs is *The Churning of the Ocean of Milk*. This work is in Angkor Wat's eastern gallery on the first level. The huge artwork is more than 150 feet (46 m) long. It illustrates a Hindu story.

In the story, a group of gods and goddesses called *devas* are searching for the potion for eternal life. They believe that it lies under an ocean of milk. They hope that by stirring the ocean, they will find it. But the devas stir for many years without finding anything. They are tired and frustrated. So they go to Vishnu for help and advice. He tells them that they should cooperate with a powerful group of demonlike beings called *asuras*. The devas and asuras have been at war with each other for many

years. But the devas agree to team up with the asuras in exchange for some of the potion. Working together, the enemies finally succeed. They also gain other wonderful things. For example, they release a group of heavenly dancers called *apsaras*. (These beings appear in many works of art throughout Angkor.) But soon after they gain the potion, fighting between the groups begins again. This constant struggle between positive and negative forces is a common theme in Hindu stories and art.

CLEARING THE WAY

In the early 1900s, the EFEO and Cambodia's government cooperate in setting up a new organization. The Conservation d'Angkor (Angkor Conservation) begins in 1908. This group dedicates itself to maintaining and protecting the great ruins in Angkor. It works closely with the EFEO.

The first Angkor Conservation leader (called a curator) is Jean Commaille. He soon sets his teams to work on the huge job of freeing Angkor's monuments from the jungle's grip. The tropical plants here grow very quickly. A *New York Times* article says, "The power of vegetation in this region is amazing, and great trees or tiny plants . . . grow with immense vigor." Another writer describes trees with "roots . . . the size of an elephant's legs."

Over the years, all these plants have taken a heavy toll on the area's buildings. In some places, vines and tree roots choke the ruins. Commaille directs workers to clear away the jungle's growth. The weather is hot and humid. The workers toil in the heat to reveal Angkor's ancient stones.

Time has been especially hard on the soft sandstone that makes up so many of Angkor's buildings. Vines and tree roots cling to some walls and columns. The pressure the plants place on the stone has cracked it in places. Sandstone also absorbs water. As the stone takes in moisture, it can swell and break. Carved sandstone is especially delicate. It sometimes flakes or peels. This kind of decay puts some of Angkor's reliefs at great risk.

Commaille and his workers are very careful as they cut and pull away the twisting and grasping plants. As they remove these webs of growth, they reveal even more reliefs and inscriptions. Commaille studies the carvings carefully. He begins to think that Khmer artists must have used special tools to create such detailed and precise works. After all, there is no way to erase or correct a picture made of stone. He eventually suggests that Angkor's artists might have used some sort of stencils (cutout patterns to trace or fill in). Commaille also writes a guide to Angkor's sites.

In 1916 armed robbers kill Jean Commaille. The curator's fellow workers are shocked and saddened. They bury Commaille near the Bayon monuments. But work at the site must go on. The Angkor Conservation begins seeking a new leader.

Jungle plants grow on and around a temple gate at Angkor in 1899. This picture was taken by Gabriel Veyre, a photographer who became famous for his images of remote locations around the world.

CHAPTER four

"The Father of Angkor"

In 1917 the new head of the Angkor Conservation, Henri Marchal, arrives in Angkor. Marchal is an expert in arts and architecture. He has also worked in Cambodia for more than ten years. He is familiar with local language, building styles, and history.

Marchal picks up where Commaille left off. He directs teams clearing the jungle away from monuments. In some ways, Marchal's work is like Mouhot's work in the previous century. He brings greater attention to the amazing ruins here. In the 1920s, many more people come to the site. They are tourists on vacation in Cambodia. They flock to Angkor, eager to see the amazing buildings they've heard and read about.

Meanwhile, various projects at Angkor continue. Two French scholars named Louis Finot and Georges Coedès have arrived at the site. Finot is an archaeologist who has studied Sanskrit. Coedès is also an expert in Sanskrit and other ancient languages. Although earlier scholars at the site translated many inscriptions, many more writings are still a mystery. And not all of them are in Sanskrit. Some of the engravings on Angkor's buildings are written in the Khmer language. As Coedès explains, "From the beginning, [the Khmers] simultaneously used two languages." These two were "a scholarly language, Sanskrit, reserved for the [family history] of royalty . . . and a common language, Khmer or Cambodian."

Coedès translates many inscriptions in both languages. He translates some writings that no earlier archaeologists or historians have figured out. His translations give researchers the most exact dates yet for when different Khmer kings reigned. They also provide more details about those reigns. A *New York Times* article in 1930 says that these carvings "reveal a king whose reign was as fabulous as any in . . . legends."

The same article in the *New York Times* describes the great difficulties facing workers at Angkor. "Angkor had been deserted for long centuries. Enormous trees had sprung up among towers and courtyards, and . . . the

"One can never look upon [Angkor Wat] without a thrill, a pause, a feeling of being caught up to the heavens. Perhaps it is the most impressive sight in the world of [buildings]."

—Helen Churchill Candee, *Angkor the Magnificent*, 1924

A Woman's Voice

Helen Churchill Candee was one of the first women to publish writings about Angkor. Born in New York City in 1858, Candee believed strongly in women's rights during a time when these views were not very popular. She was a writer and an interior decorator. She was also a survivor of the 1912 sinking of the *Titanic* and a former wartime nurse. During World War I (1914–1918), she cared for wounded soldiers in Italy. One of her patients was the famous writer Ernest Hemingway. After the war, she traveled in Asia. One of her stops was Angkor, and in 1924, she published a book called *Angkor the Magnificent*.

pressure of their growth had split the solid masonry [brickwork] until it fell in tangled confusion. Undergrowth and tropical rains had destroyed all written records."

But the workers keep pushing on through these difficulties. And Marchal has a new idea for restoring the monuments.

PICKING UP THE PIECES

About 1931 Marchal and his team begin using a restoration method called anastylosis. Marchal and other EFEO members learned this tool from Dutch archaeologists working in Indonesia. One anastylosis expert describes the process as the "rebuilding of a monument with its own materials and according to its own methods of construction." It is a way of rebuilding and restoring buildings that have partly or completely fallen down.

Marchal and his team begin using the method at Banteay Srei. This Hindu temple complex lies near the edge of the Angkor area, about 20 miles (32 km) northeast of Angkor Wat. Banteay Srei was built around the late 900s. First, workers very carefully study how and where the Banteay Srei temple and its monuments have crumbled. They look at where fallen stones have landed. They take many detailed notes about the

The Banteay Srei temple complex is dedicated to the Hindu god Shiva. Compared to Angkor Wat and Angkor Thom, it is very small. However, it houses many beautiful carvings.

positions of stones lying on the ground or on top of other stones. Then they use this information to figure out how to replace these stones. Finally, they start the rebuilding process. Sometimes this involves taking apart portions of a building before putting it back together. But the aim is always to stay true to the original architecture and building style. Marchal and his team begin training Cambodian workers to help them with this restoration process.

Marchal resigns as the Angkor Conservation leader in 1933. He has held the challenging job for more than fifteen years, and it is time for a break. But he does not stay away from Angkor for long. In 1935 Marchal returns for another two years as curator. He soon turns his attention to a new challenge at Angkor. In a set of buildings called the Bakong complex, parts of the stone roofs have begun to fall down. EFEO workers must use concrete and wood to support the crumbling structure. Marchal's workers also use anastylosis at the Bayon site and at Baphuon (a Hindu temple from the 1000s).

In 1937 Marchal steps down again as curator at Angkor. Maurice Glaize takes over as head of the conservation group. Like Marchal, Glaize and his workers use anastylosis to restore many of the monuments. Glaize's own notes and records describe this painstaking process. Workers first "cleared the surroundings and removed all the vegetation, the sections of walling that still remain standing are taken down . . . with each block being numbered." Workers clean the blocks and then put them back together "with the help of numerous drawings and photographs. At the same time the stones found in the rubble which have tumbled down from the crumbling upper walls are re-assembled according to the location of their natural fall."

In all, Glaize says, the work is something like solving a jigsaw puzzle. He adds that in that puzzle, "the pieces . . . can weigh many hundreds of kilograms, sometimes tons, and the player is forbidden to remake any sculpture . . . or decoration."

Despite its challenges, anastylosis is a valuable tool in restoring Angkor's buildings. Conservation and EFEO experts use it at sites including Banteay Samre (a Hindu temple from the 1100s) and Neak Pean (a Buddhist temple from the 1100s).

Yet Glaize and his workers do not apply this method everywhere in Angkor. For example, they decide not to make major changes to the Ta Prohm temple. This Buddhist site dates back to the mid-1100s or early 1200s. Glaize explains that Ta Prohm is "one of the most imposing [temples] and the one which had best merged with the jungle, but not yet to the point of becoming a part of it." As the American travel writer Helen Churchill Candee puts it, "Ta Prohm's state of ruin is a state of beauty."

The central sanctuary of the Neak Pean temple sits on an island in the middle of an artificial pond. The sanctuary was badly damaged by a storm in 1935. Conservation experts restored it using anastylosis.

The moat at Angkor Wat reflects the colors of the evening sky.

BOOKS AND BUILDINGS

Meanwhile, news of Angkor spreads around the globe. In 1940 a British writer, Osbert Sitwell, publishes a book called *Escape with Me!* Sitwell describes Angkor as a "chief wonder of the world today, one of the summits to which human genius has aspired in stone."

Maurice Glaize also writes a book about Angkor and his team's work there. Written in French, the book was first published in Vietnam in 1944. A few years later, it was translated into English as *Guide to the Angkor*

Monuments. It is a tour guide to the structures at Angkor. It also includes information about Khmer history and culture. Georges Coedès writes an introduction for the book. He praises Glaize's knowledge of the site. He also admires Glaize's passion for taking care of Angkor. "By . . . taking apart and rebuilding the monuments during the process of anastylosis Mr. Glaize has learnt to know their secrets and, like a professor of anatomy, reveals to his readers all the details of their structure. But further, in daily contact with the ruins since 1936, he has learnt to love them."

Sunrise, Sunset

H. W. Ponder was a British writer who visited Angkor in the early 1930s. He said that "it is at sunrise and sunset that you feel its most [powerful] charm." In a 1936 book about his travels, he describes the place at these beautiful times of day.

An hour before the dawn, [go] down the road that skirts the faintly glimmering moat of Angkor Wat, before it plunges into the gloom of the forest; and then turn off, feeling your way across the terrace between the guardian lions . . . then clamber up the steep buried stairway on the eastern face of the hill, across the plateau and up the five flights of steps, to emerge . . . on to the cool high terrace with the stars above you. . . . Here at the summit it is very still. . . . All in a moment you realize that the world is no longer dark. The sanctuaries and altars on the terrace have taken shape about you . . . the kingdom of the Khmers and [its] glory . . . spreads out on every side.

The moon's white radiance and the silence are . . . far more eerie than the deep darkness of the morning. . . . With sunset, the . . . chatter of the birds and monkeys in the trees below has ceased . . . even the cicadas . . . are silent. Decidedly it is time to go . . . once on the plateau you can take your choice of crossing it among the crumbled ruins, and plunging down the straight [steep path] that was once a stairway—or the easy, winding path through the forest . . . worn by the elephants of the explorers and excavators. Either will bring you to where the twin lions sit in darkness—black now, for here the trees are too dark to let the moonlight through; and so home along the straight road between its high dark walls of forest.

"Since its [beginning] the EFEO has [tried] to keep the sites clear with the removal of vegetation and the freeing of the temple[s] from the accumulated piles of earth and rubble . . . a colossal task . . . of preventing the devouring forces of nature from destroying the work of man."

—Maurice Glaize,
from his 1944 book on Angkor

In 1947 Marchal replaces Glaize and becomes the Angkor Conservation leader yet again. He returns to his work in the jungle. A few years later, in 1952, a *New York Times* article describes Marchal's work. He "has cleared away the thick underbrush and enormous tree roots which have burst massive stone roofs and walls apart," the writer says. "He has reconstructed, stone by stone, [Angkor's] shattered arches and turrets."

Marchal has not been replacing every stone himself, of course. But he continues to guide and lead a team of talented workers and archaeologists. Dozens of workers toil at Angkor. They are dedicated to protecting the site.

Marchal tries again to retire in 1953. As he says in a *New York Times* article, "The work is getting too hard for me." He is more than seventy-five years old. And, as the *Times* article puts it, "for almost half his lifetime [he] has watched after the huge crumbling temple of Angkor."

That same year, Cambodians celebrate a huge milestone. After ninety years under French control, the nation gains its independence from France in 1953.

Meanwhile, Marchal just cannot seem to leave Angkor behind. He comes back to the city one more time in 1957. This time he does not officially lead the Angkor Commission. But he helps and advises the new curator, Jean Laur. Marchal's knowledge of the sites and his passion for saving them still make him one of the world's greatest Angkor experts.

Angkor Thom was the capital of the Khmer empire of Jayavarman VII. The walled city has several temples, including the Bayon, which is famous for these giant stone faces.

CHAPTER Five
DARK DAYS

Under Laur's leadership, workers begin to focus on the Baphuon site. But Laur resigns as Angkor Conservation leader in 1959. He hands the Baphuon project and others over to Bernard-Philippe Groslier.

CHALLENGE AND CHANGE

Groslier gets right to work. He directs a team using anastylosis at the Thommanon site. This Hindu temple is in the Angkor Thom area. It was built between the late 1000s and early 1100s. Groslier's team carries out a major restoration at this site. Brick by brick, workers carefully rebuild Thommanon. The rebuilt temple is strong and solid.

Groslier also oversees work restoring Prasat Kravan, a Hindu temple to Vishnu from the 900s. This temple needs a lot of work. The team here builds a new foundation and adds new drains to the structure.

Workers at Prasat Kravan also replace many bricks on the temple's outer walls. Experts design these bricks to look as much like the original material as possible. But the imitation bricks each have a small mark that says CA. This mark shows that Angkor Conservation workers added these new pieces.

In addition, Groslier continues the work Laur began on the Baphuon temple. Like Angkor Wat, this temple uses the Temple Mountain design. But the mountain is crumbling. Experts at the site begin the careful work of taking apart the structure before eventually rebuilding it.

About this same time, political turmoil rocks Cambodia. Different groups within the country disagree about how the nation's government should work. Some groups are Communist. Communism is a political system based on the idea of shared property. In a Communist country, the government owns all the nation's land, money, and other resources. Individuals depend on the government to give them jobs, homes, and other things that they need.

All in the Family

Through his work at Angkor, Bernard-Philippe Groslier is following in the footsteps of his father, Georges Groslier. Before his death in 1945, Georges Groslier was an expert on Khmer art, architecture, and crafts. He also designed the building and layout of Cambodia's National Museum. The museum opened in 1920 in Phnom Penh.

"Bit by bit, with the help of local Cambodian craftsmen who . . . fit the fallen rocks back into position, [French archaeologists] repaired the temples, bridges, and balustrades.

"They uncovered the sunken . . . gardens and dug out the moats around the city of Angkor Thom. They mended the stone gods . . . and pieced together millions of fragments bearing the inscriptions that unraveled the mystery of the Khmers."

—Audrey Topping, *New York Times*, 1966

Other groups are anti-Communist. Each side has friends outside of Cambodia. The Communist groups team with other Communists in North and South Vietnam. The anti-Communists receive help from the United States and South Vietnam.

Eventually the disagreements between these groups become violent. Revolts and fighting break out around the country in the late 1960s. Civil war tears Cambodia apart.

Missing Pieces

Over the years, many items have disappeared from Angkor. This problem is not new. Some of the first European explorers and archaeologists who arrived there shipped pieces back to their own countries for research. Later, some tourists took souvenirs for themselves. This practice was common in the 1800s and into the 1900s.

But problems increased after the Cambodian civil war began. During this violent time, no one was guarding the monuments closely. Some people stole statues, carvings, and other art from the site. Then they usually sneaked these pieces out of Cambodia and sold them for large amounts of money.

Looters removed the head of this apsara. Most of the artifacts remaining at Angkor Wat are too large to move easily, but some collectors will buy broken pieces.

A TRAGIC TIME

Henri Marchal dies in 1970. The EFEO and Angkor Conservation members mourn the loss of such a great leader and expert. The EFEO experts have kept working even as clashes erupt throughout Cambodia. But Groslier fears that his teams might have to abandon their projects if the fighting gets worse. He is especially worried about the Baphuon site. He directs his workers to build simple walls around the Baphuon monuments. He hopes that these walls will at least give the area some protection from the fighting if the workers are forced to leave.

In 1972 Groslier's fears come true. The conflict in Cambodia forces Groslier and many other EFEO officials to leave Angkor. A few workers stay on. They struggle to continue their work on the monuments. But they risk their lives to do so.

In 1975 the Communist Party of Kampuchea (CPK) takes control of Cambodia. Kampuchea is an ancient name for the Khmer Empire. The CPK is called the Khmer Rouge. Awful years follow for the country. Many people die under the Khmer Rouge's rule. The Communist government executes thousands of Cambodians. Officials accuse these people of being enemies of the government, but most are innocent. Other people die from starvation or from being forced to do harsh physical work.

Cambodians accused of crimes against the Khmer Rouge dig canals at a forced labor camp in the 1970s.

No one is sure exactly how many Cambodians lose their lives. Historians estimate that anywhere between 850,000 to 3 million people died in all.

During this turmoil, the Khmer Rouge forces the last workers at Angkor to leave. With no one taking care of the sites, they quickly fall back into disrepair. Once again, Cambodia's thick jungle takes over many of the monuments. Many years of work fade away. Human impact also takes a toll. Some of the war's fighters store weapons and other supplies in Angkor's monuments. Other people hide there. A bomb hits part of Angkor Wat. A few soldiers even shoot at the temple.

The Khmer Rouge falls from power in 1979. But Cambodia is still troubled. Vietnam has taken control of the nation and fighting continues.

UNCERTAINTY FOR ANGKOR

Soon after the Khmer Rouge's reign ends, a man named Pich Keo returns to Angkor. He is the Angkor Conservation's first Cambodian curator. He speaks sadly of the damage

Bullet holes left by Khmer Rouge troops scar one of the entrances to Angkor Wat.

During the Khmer Rouge's rule, jungle plants grew up around this pavilion at Angkor. When plants grow on and around such buildings, their roots can pry apart blocks of stone. This growth can destroy carvings and endanger entire structures.

he sees at the sites. "Angkor Wat is beautiful from afar but not from close up," he says.

A glimmer of hope for Angkor appears in the mid-1980s. Even though the nation is still unstable, Cambodian officials allow a group from India to work at Angkor. This team is from an organization called the Archaeological Survey of India. They begin restoring and cleaning the monuments at the site. Indian experts from the group also begin training Cambodian workers to help with the job. Around the same time, members of a conservation group from Poland come to Angkor. This team focuses on the Bayon temple group and its monuments.

But the Indian and Polish teams cannot do all the work that they would like to. They do not have enough money or supplies.

For almost twenty years, Angkor suffers from neglect and decline. Historians, archaeologists, and other observers look on in fear and sadness. They wonder if they will lose all the work of the last one hundred years.

When archaeologists returned to Angkor Wat in the mid-1980s, they cleared vegetation from the pavilion shown on page 50. The plants had completely covered the building's terrace, steps, and elegant statues. Above is the newly cleared pavilion.

CHAPTER six

A New Dawn
at Angkor

In 1989 peace talks begin in Cambodia. They make slow but steady progress. Stability begins returning to the country. As it does, workers begin returning to Angkor.

One of the first groups to arrive in 1989 is the World Monuments Fund (WMF). This organization is based in the United States. The WMF focuses its work at Preah Khan. This Buddhist temple is also called the Sacred Sword. It dates back to the late 1100s.

The WMF's leader at Preah Khan is John Sanday. He writes about Angkor's beauty and its power. He says, "The architecture of Angkor has inspired architects, artists, travelers, and dreamers from around the world."

WORLD HERITAGE

Another major group that soon gets involved at Angkor is the United Nations Educational, Scientific, and Cultural Organization (UNESCO). UNESCO is part of the United Nations (UN). The UN was formed in 1945 to help resolve international disagreements and discuss international issues.

The head of UNESCO, Federico Mayor, visits Angkor in 1991. The following year, UNESCO names Angkor a World Heritage Site. This label means that UNESCO will give the Cambodian government extra help conserving Angkor's monuments. In return, Cambodian officials agree

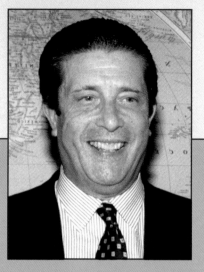

UNESCO director Federico
Mayor

"Angkor, city of the Khmer kings, is waiting to become once more the symbol of its country. . . . Yet this symbolic city is in peril. The ravages of time, the assaults of nature and the pillaging of man further its decline with every passing day. It must be saved!"

—UNESCO director Federico Mayor, 1991

follow certain rules about protecting the site. They also agree to create and follow a conservation plan.

This kind of planning is important. Archaeologists and other workers at the site constantly face questions about the safest and best ways to restore and protect Angkor. The Archaeological Survey of India's scientists and their teams at Angkor Wat use a special chemical to remove plant growth from the temple's walls and pillars. Some experts think this chemical is hurting the stone. No one really knows if this project is doing more harm than good. Observers have to keep asking these important questions.

Meanwhile, EFEO members are eager to get back to work. In 1994 some of the group's workers return to Angkor. They set about undoing the jungle's damage. They carefully remove clinging vines and leaves, just as other French workers did more than a century ago.

The next year, the Cambodian government founds a new conservation group. The organization is called the Authority for the Protection and Management of Angkor and the Region of Siem Reap (APSARA). APSARA will help oversee research and restoration in the Angkor region. The group also plans to study economic issues. For example, officials hope that tourism will increase. But they also must make sure that visitors don't harm the monuments.

And in 1996, Cambodian officials take steps to prevent any more stealing from Angkor. With help from UNESCO and the French government, the Cambodian government sets up the Heritage Police Unit. This special police force patrols and protects Angkor's buildings. Meanwhile, another group works to reclaim as many of the stolen works as possible.

French soldiers use special equipment to find and disarm land mines at the Banteay Srei temple. The Khmer Rouge and other forces planted land mines throughout the country to harm both soldiers and residents.

INTERNATIONAL TEAMWORK

As French and Cambodian groups once again work together in Angkor, they are joined by experts from other countries. For example, in 1994, Japan creates the Japanese Government Team for Safeguarding Angkor (JSA). Its workers are restoring libraries at the Bayon temple and at Angkor Wat. Like earlier groups, this team faces many difficult decisions about how to do their work. The architect Takeshi Nakagawa describes these challenges. In some cases, he says, workers have no choice but to use new sandstone to repair damage. "We use new stones only as a last resort and blend them together with old stones."

In 1996 an Italian team arrives from the International Center for Conservation in Rome (ICCROM). They begin working at Pre Rup, a Hindu temple dedicated to Shiva and built in the 900s. The Italian group faces a special challenge here. One of Pre Rup's towers is so shaky that the team fears it might fall down. To keep it from collapsing, they wrap the tower in strong wires.

A cage of metal rods surrounds and supports the fragile tower at Pre Rup temple.

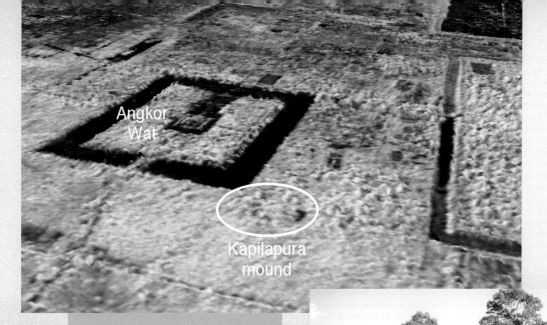

Radar images *(above)* revealed the Kapilapura mound, which covers a small city that predates Angkor Wat. In the image, forest covers the yellow areas. On the ground, the Kapilapura mound *(right)* is hard to distinguish from its surroundings.

Also in 1996, a British archaeologist named Elizabeth Moore teams up with U.S. scientists at the National Aeronautics and Space Administration (NASA). Together they use special radar to take images of Angkor from the air. These images can reveal features that the jungle hides.

What the group members see amazes them. Traces of an unseen city show up in and around Angkor Wat. As Moore studies these pictures, she begins to think the trace ruins are quite a bit older than Angkor Wat itself. They might date from the 800s—three hundred years before the great temple was built.

Moore and her team continue to study this new information. Meanwhile, they are also able to use the images to create three-dimensional maps of the site. These maps are the most detailed and precise that anyone has yet seen.

A member of the German Apsara Conservation Project squeezes glue into cracks in a relief carving.

Many more international groups soon follow. In 1997 the German Apsara Conservation Project comes to Angkor. This organization is dedicated to studying, restoring, and protecting Angkor Wat's reliefs. Its members also work to teach local Cambodian workers to continue this project. In 2000 a group from China's Cultural Relics Bureau begins work at Chau Say Tevoda, a Hindu temple dating from the late 1000s to mid-1100s.

The following year, a Japanese group from Tokyo's Sophia University makes a huge discovery at Banteay Kdei. At this Buddhist temple complex, the team finds 274 pieces of statues and other sculpture. They appear to be from Buddhist artworks. Historians believe that Khmer Buddhists may have buried these pieces in about the 1200s. Their goal might have been to protect them from Hindus who wanted to destroy Buddhist symbols.

Also in 2001, the JSA from Japan begins a new project. Prasat Suor Prat is a group of twelve towers at Angkor Thom. Historians are not sure what these towers were for. Were they for worship? Were they to

The twelve towers of Prasat Suor Prat remain a mystery. A Chinese visitor in the thirteenth century wrote that they were used as courts in legal disputes. But no records of the buildings' purpose remain from the years they were in use.

hold treasures belonging to the king? Maybe they were for government ceremonies. So far no one knows. So, the JSA simply gets to work restoring them. Team members take down parts of the structures. They repair some of the stone bricks before using them to rebuild. Sometimes, they need to make new bricks.

A new team from the Archaeological Survey of India arrives in 2004. They begin working at Ta Prohm. Like earlier workers at this temple, the team does not plan to remove the giant trees that surround the monuments. They will work around them to restore parts of Ta Prohm.

Taming the Land

How did Angkor's people feed themselves? This is another question the workers at the site ask. The ancient people seem to have been farmers. But how did they grow any crops in the area's thick forests?

Over time, the people studying Angkor put together a picture of the past. Seasonal storms called monsoons bring heavy rains that flood the Mekong River each year. This rush of water swells the Tonle Sap Lake. Khmer farmers needed this water during dry periods. They built canals running from the lake to their fields. With this watering system, they were able to grow rice and other grains all year round.

Year-round food production helped the Khmer Empire and its people become powerful. That power faded long ago. But the archaeologists and historians at Angkor can still sense it. They see it in the great buildings all around them.

Tonle Sap Lake still provides many small Cambodian villages with water for farming. It is also a rich source of fish.

ANOTHER GLIMPSE INTO THE PAST

In 2007 an international team releases new radar images of Angkor Wat. These sharp pictures show that the Angkor settlement is much larger than anyone knew. The pictures show the outlines of at least seventy-four more temples. The images reveal the paths of many more canals. This shows that the Khmer watering system for farming was larger than anyone had seen before. In addition, they show that more than one thousand ponds created by local people dotted the area. All together,

"There are few places in the world where one feels proud to be a member of the human race, and one of these is certainly Angkor. . . . One does not need to be a Buddhist or a Hindu to understand. You need only let yourself go."

—Italian author Tiziano Terzani, 1997

the entire settlement may have covered as much as 1,150 square miles (2,978 sq. km) and perhaps more. That size makes it similar to modern Los Angeles or New York City.

This information gives historians new clues about what caused Angkor's civilization to collapse. Some experts think that Khmer farmers may have put too much pressure on the land and the water systems. At first, being able to grow so many crops and feed so many people was a huge advantage. But historians think that at the Khmer Empire's peak, the region might have held up to one million people. Maybe this population simply grew too large for the land to support.

Workers restore a wall of relief sculpture at the Terrace of the Leper King, The name refers to a statue, thought to be of a king or god, that was found on top of the terrace.

EPILOGUE

Historians and archaeologists still can't say exactly why or how Angkor changed from a bustling city to a vast set of ruins. They still are not sure how Khmer artists created some of the great works here. And the meaning of some of these statues and carvings is not clear yet. Many mysteries remain. But each day of work at the site brings new clues and new knowledge. The quest to solve Angkor's puzzles goes on.

Meanwhile, Angkor has become one of Asia's greatest tourist attractions. Hundreds of thousands of international visitors come to see this amazing site each year.

Many thousands of Cambodians also visit Angkor every year. Cambodians take great pride in these monuments. Angkor Wat is Cambodia's national symbol. It has appeared on national flags since 1863. And it is still an

A tourist climbs the steps of Phnom Bakeng temple. The number of visitors to Angkor has increased as the political situation in Cambodia becomes more stable.

Buddhist monks take refuge from the sun in the shade of Angkor Wat temple.

important religious site. Buddhist monks continue to visit the temple to pay their respects. Wearing bright orange robes, they dot Angkor's grounds. The monks form a link to Angkor's majestic past as they honor traditions of worship that are hundreds of years old. For these and millions of other visitors, Angkor still holds great power. It is a treasure for the whole world to value and to protect.

THE TEMPLES OF ANGKOR

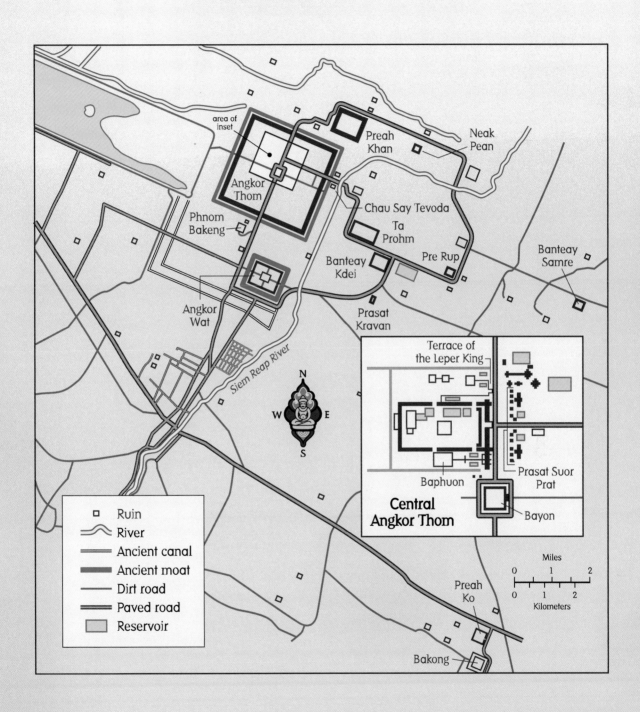

area of inset

Preah Khan

Neak Pean

Angkor Thom

Phnom Bakeng

Chau Say Tevoda

Ta Prohm

Pre Rup

Banteay Samre

Banteay Kdei

Prasat Kravan

Angkor Wat

Siem Reap River

N
W   E
S

Terrace of the Leper King

Baphuon

Prasat Suor Prat

Bayon

Central Angkor Thom

☐ Ruin
〜 River
═ Ancient canal
▬ Ancient moat
— Dirt road
═ Paved road
▨ Reservoir

Miles
0   1   2

0   1   2
Kilometers

Preah Ko

Bakong

TIMELINE

500s B.C.
Buddhism begins in India.

100s B.C
Hinduism becomes a major religion in India.

A.D. 802
Jayavarman II becomes king of the entire Khmer Empire. He declares the realm's independence and names himself a god-king.

1113–1150
Suryavarman II rules. His builders begin work on Angkor Wat during his reign.

LATE 1100s
Jayavarman VII's workers begin building Angkor Thom as a new capital.

1296
The Chinese traveler Zhou Daguan visits Angkor and stays for one year.

1300s–1400s
The Khmer Empire's power declines, and Angkor eventually collapses.

1431
Thai armies attack and conquer Angkor.

1860
Henri Mouhot first sees Angkor.

1863
Cambodia becomes a French protectorate.

1917
Henri Marchal, the father of Angkor, takes over the Angkor Conservation.

1930s
Marchal's teams begin using anastylosis to restore Angkor's sites.

1953
Cambodia gains its independence from France.

1967
Civil war begins in Cambodia.

1975–1979
The Khmer Rouge holds power.

1989
Peace talks to end the fighting in Cambodia begin.

1992
Angkor becomes a UNESCO World Heritage site.

1994
L'École Française d'Extrême-Orient (EFEO) workers return after the war.

2001
Japanese workers at Banteay Kdei discover 274 pieces of buried sculpture.

2007
New radar images show that the Angkor site is even larger than experts had thought.

2008
Experts warn that huge numbers of visitors to Angkor are placing great stress on the monuments and the land.

GLOSSARY

anastylosis: a method of restoring and rebuilding archaeological sites. The method aims to re-create historical sites in a way that matches their original form. The process includes studying how a site has collapsed and using original building materials when possible. Sometimes workers take apart a building before putting it back together.

archaeology: the study of human history using clues such as ruins and ancient objects

architecture: the design and building style of structures

Buddhism: a religion founded in India by the monk Siddhartha Gautama (the Buddha, or "the Enlightened One") in the 500s B.C. Buddhism reached the Khmer Empire about the A.D. 900s. Some of Buddhism's central ideas focus on searching for understanding and knowledge, giving up worldly things, and leading a life of goodness and wisdom.

Communism: a political system based on the idea of common, rather than private, property. In a Communist system, the government controls resources and distributes them equally among citizens.

conservation: the action, or process, of protecting something valuable

curator: a leader or person in charge of a project

gopura: a decorated gateway building in Khmer architecture

Hinduism: an ancient religion that became important in India in the 100s B.C. Hindus believe in many gods and goddesses that influence human lives. Hindus also believe that positive and negative forces are constantly struggling for power in the universe and in people.

inscription: written words. At Angkor, archaeologists study inscriptions that are carved into stone.

Khmer: a people, a language, and an ancient empire all centered in Cambodia. The Khmer language is still the national language of Cambodia.

missionary: a religious worker. Missionaries often travel to other countries to spread information about and convert people to their religions.

monsoon: a seasonal windstorm that brings heavy rains

protectorate: a nation or region that is under the control of an outside power

relief: a three-dimensional picture carved into a wall or other flat surface

Sanskrit: a language used in ancient India and other parts of Southeast Asia

Temple Mountain: an architecture style that many Khmer designers used at Angkor. The Temple Mountain represents Mount Meru, home of the Hindu gods and goddesses.

PRONUNCIATION GUIDE

No one knows exactly how to pronounce Sanskrit words. In modern times, this ancient language only exists in written form. But Khmer is still Cambodia's national language. Below is a pronunciation key to some of the Khmer words and names used in the text.

Angkor	ANG-kor
Angkor Wat	ANG-kor WAHT
Banteay Srei	BAHN-tay SHREE
gopura	GOH-pur-uh
Groslier	grohz-lee-AY
Keo	KEY-oh
Khmer	kuh-MEHR
Khmer Rouge	kuh-MEHR roozh
Marchal	mar-SHAHL
Mouhot	moo-OH
Preah Kahn	PRAY KAHN

WHO'S WHO?

Bernard-Philippe Groslier (1926–1986) was born in Cambodia. His father, Georges Groslier, was a respected architect and expert on Khmer art and history. Bernard-Philippe Groslier went on to study Khmer history, and he became the Angkor Conservation's leader after Jean Laur resigned in 1959. He oversaw many projects at Angkor, but he had to leave in 1972 during the Khmer Rouge's rule.

Pich Keo is an art historian and a former assistant of Bernard-Philippe Groslier. He survived the Khmer Rouge's harsh rule during the 1970s and in the 1990s went on to become the Angkor Conservation's first Cambodian leader. He also served as the director of Cambodia's National Museum for several years.

Henri Marchal (1876–1970) was born in Paris, France. He studied architecture and archaeology there before going to Cambodia in 1905. After Jean Commaille's death, Marchal became the Angkor Conservation curator in 1917. He was the first to use anastylosis to restore the monuments. He spent more than fifty years working on and off at Angkor. He died in 1970 at Siem Reap City, Cambodia.

Henri Mouhot (1826–1861) was born in Montbéliard, France, in 1826. He was a scientist and an explorer. In 1860 he went to Cambodia on a mission from Britain's Royal Geographical Society and Zoological Society. His goal was to gather samples of plants in Southeast Asia. But his most famous work was his writings about the ruins he saw at Angkor. Mouhot died of a fever while traveling in Laos. But his writings lived on. They informed many more people about Angkor.

SOURCE NOTES

9 Jon Ortner, *Angkor: Celestial Temples of the Khmer Empire* (New York: Abbeville Press Publishers, 2002), 9.

9 Michael D. Coe, *Angkor and the Khmer Civilization* (New York: Thames & Hudson, 2003), 11.

10 Charles Higham, *The Civilization of Angkor* (Berkeley: University of California Press, 2001), 2.

10 Coe, *Angkor and the Khmer Civilization,* 13.

11 Richard Covington, "Rescuing Angkor," *Smithsonian Magazine,* February 2004, http://www.smithsonianmagazine .com/issues/2004/february/angkor.php (August 16, 2007).

11 Osbert Sitwell, *Escape with Me! An Oriental Sketch-Book* (New York: Harrison-Hilton Books, 1940), 69.

11 Venerable Vodano Sophan Seng, "Brief Presentation to a Volunteer Group of Glenbow Museum in the Asian Gallery," *Cambodian View: Perspectives and Paradigm Shifts,* May 28, 2005, http://www.cambodianview .com/documents/articles/Brief _Presentation.pdf (January 3, 2008).

12 Higham, *The Civilization of Angkor,* 3.

17 Dawn Rooney, *Angkor: Cambodia's Wondrous Khmer Temples. (*Sheung Wan, Hong Kong: Odyssey Books and Guides, 2006; Distributed in the United States by Norton & Company), 49.

17 New York Times Company, "The Ruins of the Great Temple at Angkor," *New York Times,* May 10, 1874, http://query .nytimes.com/gst/abstract.html?res=9B 02E4D81338EE3BBC4852DFB366838F6 69FDE (October 3, 2007).

17 Ibid.

17 Rooney, *Angkor,* 167.

20 L. J. Robbins, "Fabulous Angkor Reveals Its Secrets," *New York Times,* March 2, 1930, http://select.nytimes .com/gst/abstract.html?res=F30815FF 3B5D157A93C0A91788D85F448385F9 (October 3, 2007).

24 Maurice Glaize, *The Monuments of the Angkor Group,* 2003, http://www .theangkorguide.com/images/ download/angkor-guide.pdf (January 3, 2008), 37.

25 Robbins, "Fabulous Angkor Reveals Its Secrets."

30 Ibid.

32 New York Times Company, "In South-Eastern Asia," *New York Times,* October 10, 1881, http://query.nytimes .com/gst/abstract.html?res=9D07E2D81 53BE033A25753C1A9669D94609FD7CF (January 3, 2008).

32 Anabel I. Janssen, "Jungle Trip to See the Ruins of Angkor Wat," *New York Times,* May 5, 1957, http://select

.nytimes.com/gst/abstract.html?res=F2
0C1FFE3D55137A93C7A9178ED85F438
585F9 (October 3, 2007).

35 Glaize, *The Monuments of the Angkor
    Group*, 20.

36 Randy Bryan Bigham, "Life's Décor: A
    Biography of Helen Churchill Candee,"
    Encyclopedia Titanica, 2006, http://
    www.encyclopedia-titanica.org/articles/
    candee_01.php (January 3, 2008).

36 Robbins, "Fabulous Angkor Reveals Its
    Secrets."

36 Ibid.

37 Glaize, *The Monuments of the Angkor
    Group*, 66.

38 Ibid.

39 Ibid.

39 Ibid., 155.

39 Rooney, *Angkor*, 300.

40 Ibid., 114.

40 Ibid.

40 Ibid., 118.

41 Sitwell, *Escape*, 69.

42 Glaize, *The Monuments of the Angkor
    Group*, 5.

42 Ibid., 66.

42 Peggy Durdin, "Angkor's Past
    Recaptured," *New York Times*, June
    22, 1952, http://select.nytimes.com/gst/
    abstract.html?res=F40D10FF3A58107A
    93C0AB178DD85F468585F9 (October 3,
    2007).

42 New York Times Company, "Ruins of
    Cambodia Await New Touch," *New
    York Times*, April 21, 1952, http://select
    .nytimes.com/gst/abstract.html?res=FB
    0614FC3C5E177B93C3AB178FD85F468
    585F9 (October 3, 2007).

42 Rooney, *Angkor*, 56.

43 William E. Fisher, "To Unknown Indo-
    China," *New York Times*, June 4, 1939,
    http://select.nytimes.com/gst/abstract
    .html?res=F60E12F93A58127A93C6A91
    78DD85F4D8385F9 (October 3, 2007).

46 Audrey R. Topping, "Cambodia's Great
    Temple City in the Jungle," *New York
    Times*, March 20, 1966, http://select
    .nytimes.com/gst/abstract.html?res=F1
    0A16FF3E5C15768FDDA90A94DB405B
    868AF1D3 (October 3, 2007).

50 Henry Kamm, "Looting and Graffiti
    Eat Away at the Treasure of Angkor,"
    New York Times, April 15, 1980, http://
    select.nytimes.com/gst/abstract.html?
    res=F10C13FD3E5F13778DDDAC0994D
    C405B8084F1D3 (October 3, 2007).

53 Ortner, *Angkor*, 170.

54 Rooney, *Angkor*, 61–62.

56 Covington, "Rescuing Angkor."

60 Tiziano Terzani, *A Fortune-Teller Told
    Me: Earthbound Travels in the Far East*
    (New York: Harmony Books, 2001), 236.

SELECTED BIBLIOGRAPHY

Coe, Michael D. *Angkor and the Khmer Civilization*. New York: Thames & Hudson, 2003.

Covington, Richard. "Rescuing Angkor." *Smithsonian Magazine*. February 2004. http://www.smithsonianmagazine.com/issues/2004/february/angkor.php (August 16, 2007).

Durdin, Peggy. "Angkor's Past Recaptured." *New York Times*. June 22, 1952. http://select.nytimes.com/gst/abstract.html?res =F40D10FF3A58107A93C0AB178DD85F468585F9 (October 3, 2007).

Fisher, William E. "To Unknown Indo-China." *New York Times*. June 4, 1939. http://select.nytimes.com/gst/abstract.html?res =F60E12F93A58127A93C6A9178DD85F4D8385F9 (October 3, 2007).

Glaize, Maurice. *The Monuments of the Angkor Group*. 2003. http://www .theangkorguide.com/ (October 3, 2007).

Higham, Charles. *The Civilization of Angkor*. Berkeley: University of California Press, 2001.

Hornik, Richard. "The Battle of Angkor." *Time.com*. April 6, 1992. http:// www.time.com/time/magazine/article/0,9171,975237,00.html (October 3, 2007).

Janssen, Anabel I. "Jungle Trip to See the Ruins of Angkor Wat." *New York Times*. May 5, 1957. http://select.nytimes.com/gst/abstract.html ?res=F20C1FFE3D55137A93C7A9178ED85F438585F9 (October 3, 2007).

Kamm, Henry. "Looting and Graffiti Eat Away at the Treasure of Angkor." *New York Times*. April 15, 1980. http://select.nytimes.com/gst/abstract .html?res=F10C13FD3E5F13778DDDAC0994DC405B8084F1D3 (October 3, 2007).

New York Times Company. "Ruins of Cambodia Await New Touch." *New York Times*. April 21, 1952. http://select.nytimes.com/gst/abstract.html ?res=FB0614FC3C5E177B93C3AB178FD85F468585F9 (October 3, 2007).

———. "The Ruins of the Great Temple at Angkor." *New York Times*. May 10, 1874. http://query.nytimes.com/gst/abstract.html?res =9B02E4D81338EE3BBC4852DFB366838F669FDE (October 3, 2007).

Ortner, Jon. *Angkor: Celestial Temples of the Khmer Empire*. New York: Abbeville Press Publishers, 2002.

Robbins, L. J. "Fabulous Angkor Reveals Its Secrets." *New York Times*. March 2, 1930. http://select.nytimes.com/gst/abstract.html?res =F30815FF3B5D157A93C0A91788D85F448385F9 (October 3, 2007).

Rooney, Dawn. *Angkor: Cambodia's Wondrous Khmer Temples*. Sheung Wan, Hong Kong: Odyssey Books and Guides, 2006. Distributed in the United States by Norton & Company.

Shenon, Philip. "Washing Buddha's Face." *New York Times*. June 21, 1992. http://query.nytimes.com/gst/fullpage.html?res =9E0CE6DD153DF932A15755C0A964958260 (October 3, 2007).

Sitwell, Osbert. *Escape with Me! An Oriental Sketch-Book*. New York: Harrison-Hilton Books, 1940.

Terzani, Tiziano. *A Fortune-Teller Told Me: Earthbound Travels in the Far East*. New York: Harmony Books, 2001.

Topping, Audrey R. "Cambodia's Great Temple City in the Jungle." *New York Times*. March 20, 1966. http://select.nytimes.com/gst/abstract .html?res=F10A16FF3E5C15768FDDA90A94DB405B868AF1D3 (October 3, 2007).

FURTHER READING AND WEBSITES

BOOKS

Deedrick, Tami. *Khmer Empire*. Austin, TX: Raintree Steck-Vaughn, 2002.

Goldstein, Margaret J. *Cambodia in Pictures*. Minneapolis: Twenty-First Century Books, 2004.

Orna-Ornstein, John. *Archaeology: Discovering the Past*. New York: Oxford University Press, 2002.

Spagnoli, Cathy, and Lina Mao Wall. *Judge Rabbit and the Tree Spirit: A Folktale from Cambodia*. San Francisco: Children's Book Press, 1991.

WEBSITES:

The Angkor Guide
http://theangkorguide.com/
Download a copy of Maurice Glaize's book about the Angkor Monuments at this site.

Angkor's Ancient Enormity Uncovered
http://news.nationalgeographic.com/news/2007/08/photogalleries/
Angkor-pictures/index.html
This site from National Geographic includes a photo gallery focusing on recent finds at Angkor. Also visit http://video.nationalgeographic.com/video/player/places/culture-places/buildings-landmarks/cambodia_angkor.html to see a short video about Angkor.

Angkor: World Heritage Centre
http://whc.unesco.org/en/list/668
This site from UNESCO offers a gallery of images of Angkor. It also includes a map of the region and an overview of the site.

APSARA—Temples and Sites

http://www.autoriteapsara.org/en/angkor/temples_sites.html

Click on this map to get more information about individual sites and monuments at Angkor. The APSARA site also offers information about the history, art, and restoration of Angkor.

World Heritage Tour: Angkor

http://www.world-heritage-tour.org/asia/kh/angkor/map.html

Take a three-dimensional virtual tour of Angkor Wat and other sites in the Angkor area at this site.

INDEX

ABOUT THE AUTHOR

Alison Behnke is an author and editor of books for young people. Among her other books are *The Conquests of Alexander the Great, The Conquests of Genghis Khan,* and *Kim Jong Il's North Korea.* She enjoys reading, writing, and traveling, and she lives in Rome, Italy.

PHOTO ACKNOWLEDGMENTS

The images in this book are used with permission of: © Tang Chhin Sothy/AFP/Getty Images, p. 4; © Hulton Archive/Getty Images, p. 5; © Laura Westlund/Independent Picture Service, pp. 7, 65; © French School/Bibliotheque des Arts Decoratifs, Paris, France, Archives Charmet/The Bridgeman Art Library, p. 8; © Royal Geographical Society, London, UK/The Bridgeman Art Library, p. 13; © Adoc-photos/Art Resource, NY, pp. 14, 33; © Fredrik Naumann/Panos Pictures, pp. 16, 47; Library of Congress, p. 19 (LC-USZ62-96743); © Eliot Elisofon/Time & Life Pictures/Getty Images, p. 21; © Ken McIaren/Art Directors, p. 22; © Luca I. Tettoni/CORBIS, pp. 24, 30; © Kevin R. Morris/CORBIS, pp. 26–27, 62; © Michael Freeman/CORBIS, p. 28; © Darryl Villaret/Alamy, p. 29; © Robert Preston/Alamy, p. 31; © age fotostock/SuperStock, pp. 32, 60; © Matthew Wakem/Aurora/Getty Images, p. 34; © Wendy Connett/Alamy, pp. 37, 39; © Steve L. Raymer/National Geographic/Getty Images, pp. 40–41; © Gina Martin/National Geographic/Getty Images, p. 44; © STR/AFP/Getty Images, p. 48; © Tony Roddam/Alamy, p. 49; © Wilbur E. Garrett/National Geographic/Getty Images, pp. 50, 52; AP Photo/Michel Lipchitz, p. 54; © Catherine Karnow/CORBIS, p. 55; © Joson/zefa/CORBIS, p. 56; NASA/JPL, p. 57 (top); Photograph courtesy of Dr. Elizabeth Moore, Department of Art and Archaeology, School of Oriental and African Studies, University of London, p. 57 (bottom); © LOOK Die Bildagentur der Fotografen GmbH/Alamy, p. 58; © Craig Lovell/Eagle Visions Photography/Alamy, p. 59; AP Photo/David Longstreath, p. 63; AP Photo/Richard Vogel, p. 64.

Front Cover: © John McDermott/Asia Images/Getty Images.